SIMULTANEOUSLY II

Simultaneously II
Copyright © 2024 by Christina Trezevant McGriff

Published in the United States of America

Library of Congress Control Number: 2024920084
ISBN   Paperback: 979-8-89091-724-9
ISBN   Hardback: 979-8-89091-725-6
ISBN   eBook: 979-8-89091-726-3

All rights reserved. No part of this publication may be reproduced, stored in a retrieval system or transmitted in any way by any means, electronic, mechanical, photocopy, recording or otherwise without the prior permission of the author except as provided by USA copyright law.

The opinions expressed by the author are not necessarily those of ReadersMagnet, LLC.

ReadersMagnet, LLC
10620 Treena Street, Suite 230 | San Diego, California, 92131 USA
1.619. 354. 2643 | www.readersmagnet.com

Book design copyright © 2024 by ReadersMagnet, LLC. All rights reserved.

Cover design by Christina McGriff
Interior design by Ched Celiz

SIMULTANEOUSLY II

Written by
Christina Trezevant McGriff

A book that compares the Biden's administration with the Trump administration, and reports on SCOTUS and multiple 2024 salient issues. A lot was happening in "real time" as we journeyed through our most consequential election for the United States' 47th president.

ReadersMagnet, LLC

INTRODUCTION

Technology has allowed us to access more simultaneously in and around the world. Covid19 blew in like a Tsunami in 2019, and officially ended in the US on May 11, 2023. The origin of the virus has yet to be confirmed.

Artificial Intelligence, (no human conscience) is being recommended and used to reduce cost, time, and multiple issues in need of solutions. Ongoing critical implementation of mechanisms is paramount to prevent machines from making decisions that only humans should discern.

The rise of social media platforms such Snap Chat, TikTok, Instagram, and especially iPad usage has scientifically been proven to reduce sleep levels, personal movement, and social interactions which has developed into a Public Health concern that causes anxiety, depression, and isolation.

To date, we are simultaneously witnessing the #47th presidential campaign between #45 Trump and #46 Biden, who are both running for a 2nd term. Trump is now a convicted felon awaiting sentencing, and full official immunity has been awarded to Trump by six conservative justices, while three liberal justices dissented. On 07/20/24, a bullet hit #45 outer ear while hosting a rally in Butler, PA. The sniper was a 20 yr. old republican who killed a father and was consequently shot and killed by the secret service for an assassination attempt.

I made a commitment to write Simultaneous II to compare the Bidens' administration with the Trumps' administration. My reason also for authoring the book was to leave my grandsons, Phoenix 11, and Amir 5, a glimpse of history through the eyes of their Nana in 2024. All three books From Small to Tall, Simultaneously, and Simultaneously II are available on Amazon, Barnes & Noble Bookstore, and Readers Magnet LLC. These titles are also available in the Library of Congress to retrieve and share at any time.

TABLE OF CONTENTS

INTRODUCTION 5
AFFIRMATIVE ACTION 8
AFGHANISTAN 10
AIRLINES 12
ALL OUR MIGHT 14
ALL YOUR HEART, SOUL, AND MIND 16
AMERICA'S GREAT RESIGNATION 18
ARTIFICIAL INTELLIGENCE (AI) 20
BIDEN'S APOLOGY 22
BIDEN'S BILLS PASSED 24
BIDEN AND CLIMATE CONTROL 26
BIDEN AND CORPORATIONS 28
BLACK LIVES MATTER (BLM) 30
BLACKS AND VP HARRIS 32
BLM: THE COLD WAR 34
BORDER CONTROL 36
CITIZEN TRUMP 38
CLASSIFIED DOCUMENTS 40
CLIMATE 42
CLIMATE CULTURE 44
CODE RED (CLIMATE) 46
CONSTITUTION (PART I) 48
CONSTITUTION (PART II) 50
COVID CONTINUED 52
COVID PANDEMIC ENDS 54
CRITICAL RACE THEORY (CRT) 56
DEBT CEILING 58
DEMOCRACY 60
DOMESTIC VIOLENCE 62
ELECTORAL COLLEGE 64
FULLY VACCINATED 66

GLOBALIZATION	68
GLOBAL INNOVATIONS	70
GREAT RESIGNATION	72
GUN VIOLENCE I	74
GUN VIOLENCE II	76
HAITI	78
HAPPINESS	80
IMMIGRATION	82
IMMUNITY	84
INCLUSIVITY	86
INDICTMENTS OF #45	88
INFRASTRUCTURE	90
INSURRECTION	92
MAGA	94
MENTAL HEALTH	96
MOON TRIPS	98
9/11/2001 (911)	100
OPIATES	102
POLICE REFORM	104
ROE VS WADE 1	106
SCOTUS AND VACCINES	108
STATE OF THE UNION	110
TRUMP	112
TRUMP CRIMINALITIES	114
TRUMP AND THE DOJ	116
TRUMP IMPEACHMENTS	118
TRUTH IN OCOEE, FLORIDA	120
TWENTY TWENTY-THREE (2023)	122
TWO AMERICAS	124
WAR	126
WITHDRAWAL	128

AFFIRMATIVE ACTION

Leviticus 24:22
You shall have the same rule for the sojourner
and for the native, for I am the Lord your God

Scotus Ketanji Brown Jackson rejected the idea of a reversed Affirmative Action ruling
Theoretical perceptions and actualities are two consequentially different schoolings
It was designed to include and sustain marginalized groups within the workforce
With the protection of feds, successful advancements grew when law took its' course

This new law was pivotal in facilitating equal employment opportunities for all races
In 1965, Pres. Johnson halted discrimination due to sex, religion, or race in federal spaces
In 1970, Pres. Nixon directed agencies to include minorities contracts or be put on notice
In 2023, after unfair practices hearings, AA was reversed by #45 stacked SCOTUS

The message was clear that 62 years of minorities considerations was here, but now gone
Backward movements fueled systematic racism, with no protection from negative harm
After 400 yrs. of inequalities, justice denied by human design was the message sent
We pay the salaries of legislators who have selfish agendas is what the setback meant

As of now, new-born have less freedom than the 55+ community recently had
The reversal of a "fair +equal" law is part of Project 25 scheme that smells really bad
No affirmative action, rights to abort, black history teachings, and the list will grow
It's a crystal-clear picture of who will get what, if #46 loses, it becomes #45's show

AFGHANISTAN

Deuteronomy 32:32
For their vine comes from the vine of Gomorra. Their grapes are grapes of poison and clusters are bitter

The piped in music stopped as the US troops withdrew in 2021 in 100+ weather
The new regime returned the country to its old Taliban customs and endeavors
It consisted completely of men as all women rights was reversed and banned
A 20-year US investment failed the females as male rights continued to stand

US received Intel when positioned from within put the new info to a test
Al Qaeda falsely bolstered victory within their own country's political unrest
Russia, China, and Pakistan negotiated with them without the US on board
Afghans desperately needed the US resources that they could not afford

20 years of protection and monetary support aimed to sustain humanitarian rights
US servicemen reported leaders inside the culture were always on a different plight
False facades with English signs as women were temporarily allowed to be schooled
Was seen as an "appearance only deals" to ramp up supplies from the global pool

After the US withdrawal, the Afghans recalibrated without hesitation and force
Mixed concerns of resistance from women percolated and took its' own new course
The US intervened for 20 years to create a culture of a shared unified democracy
Afghans belief systems remained ingrained, as they returned to a familiar autocracy

AIRLINES

Isaiah 60:8
Who are these that fly as a cloud, and as doves to their windows

Air travel schedules was unpredictable as higher rates of employees called out
Covid continued its 2nd year spread globally with mixed critiques throughout
Covid affected over 5K staff members retiring or resigning as they wanted out
Without previous flight knowledge, training time was <u>the delay</u> it brought about

Angry passengers brawled in the <u>air</u> about masks which often went awry
Global temperaments were on <u>high alert</u> as we travelled though the skies
To wear or not to wear the <u>masks</u> was the contention the stewards controlled
These unchartered waters added to a list of Covid issues in need of patrol

The bedlam created legal fines ordered and collected into the <u>millions</u>
Mechanisms were put into place to avoid amounts rising into the trillions
Desperately needed mask mandates were <u>finally</u> put in place for air travel
Attendants for the first time were trained for <u>combat</u> when things unraveled

Everything is relative in space and time, things eventually connected to another
Covid 19 issues stretched expansively with different protocols given to recover
Very <u>scary</u> for all who lived through this infectious, uninvited, deadly stranger
<u>Simultaneously</u>, things were occurring bringing new alarms and new dangers

Weather became notably unpredictable with sudden changes in the air
Ticket costs rose to rates where most customers simply could not bare
Employees left the industry, reducing needed controllers who legally could fly
Without previous flight training, new flyers required much more time to comply

Simultaneously II

ALL OUR MIGHT

Isaiah 33:22
For the Lord is our judge, the Lord is our lawgiver,
the Lord is our King and he will save us

A party that continues to stay loyal to a man who created a cult-like following
Rules didn't matter as long as it ended in a win for Trump's mind borrowing
Borrowing of the minds of millions with gaslighting techniques and falsehoods
That encouraged separations in a democracy around information misunderstood

No sense of humility, decency, or integrity was presented by the party during his term
Leaving taxpayers and lawmakers perplexed and citizens <u>stunned</u> like a deadly germ
Depraved were the masses who were under his thumb with no benefits to themselves
A true demonic spirit, diminished the balance of peace and a stable sustaining health

Even after twice impeached, found liable of sexual abuse, with multiple on-going charges
His beguiled fan base continued to love him and deny any charges of wrongness at large
Slowly his <u>farce</u> was being proven, and the lies of #45 came into some flickering light
America was fighting to regain its' original <u>democratic vision</u> with all its' human might

This situation is dire, and the seriousness cannot be over stressed in the USA
#45 has books on how he will transform our democracy that citizens <u>must</u> obey
<u>Project 2025</u> has detailed what will be realized under #45 "Rule of **his** Law"
<u>Our Vote,</u> will be the <u>only recourse</u> that will shut him down and clamor his jaw

ALL YOUR HEART, SOUL, AND MIND

Romans 15:1
Now we who are strong ought to bear the weaknesses
of those without strength and not just please ourselves

Much time is spent seeking approval, affection, and money which is a temporary goal
King Jesus will protect everything including your precious heart, mind, and your soul
Joy and gratitude will shine each day when rejoicing with kindness and with thanks
The mind erases the darkness into a streaming light, which will place at first rank

Love the Lord with all your heart, all your mind, and all your soul...

Even now when devoting our time to what we think is important for that day
Transforms into the need in the natural, with desires from the spirit to pray
Let's give him all the honor, and glory, and invite his spirit in with a passion
Store up riches in heaven that welcomes you into his glory in natural fashions

Love the Lord with all your heart, all your mind, and all your soul...

Trusting in achievements and money is an indication of a measurement of success
But true wisdom is given freely from the Lord, and a lasting peace at its' best
Take time to be still and hear that small whisper transforming your thoughts
Forgiveness, patience, with a listening ear is what should be actively sought

Love the Lord with all your heart, all your mind, and all your soul...

AMERICA'S GREAT RESIGNATION

Proverbs 14:34
Righteousness exalts a nation,
but sin is a reproach to any people

As of 2021, over 5 million people still, do not enjoy their jobs
They re-evaluated situations and noted that their lives got robbed
Childcare issues were major for parents, when kids were sent home
Jobs increasingly needed employees while new solutions roamed

America remained divided about vaccines and wearing masks
This led to deadly consequences despite it being a simple task
The restaurant industry lost businesses and few re-opened slowly
Then along came variant Omicron that repeated closures knowingly

US Ports had pending deliveries at sea causing months of delays
The shortage of truck drivers also caused stoppage of items at bay
Biden saw a need to intervene as holiday sales were in full swing
The carriers were under pressure, as shoppers wanted Xmas things

The US was going through a massive social, political and spiritual change
Some movement remain slow, while other plans quickly were rearranged
This generations' access to new technology has evolved unlike ever before
Combinations of new ideas are taking over as AI is now inside your doors

The have and have-nots remained active with different agendas and plans
Processing simultaneously and individually was a lot to ponder and understand
While seeing this uninvited global pandemic called "CoVid 19"
The world re-adjusted urgently and was desperate for normalcy to reconvene

ARTIFICIAL INTELLIGENCE (AI)

Colossians 3:2
Set your mind on things that
are above and not things that are on earth

Artificial Intelligence is a wide-ranging tool that enables the computer to reintegrate info
It also has a built-in field of integration that makes independent suggestions flow
They behave on their own without coding commands, thus named 'artificial intelligence'
It mimics human cognition, which is a mental perception of memory and thought relevance

Integration of these systems replaces human activities with results deemed to be smart
It mastered abilities to develop changes in vehicle safety with tested innovative new parts
AI role in technology can increase the GDP by $16 trillion by 2030 across the globe
It replaces human decision making while spotting inefficiencies when setting probes

It can develop education models for employees to improve skill levels in job situations
AI also can reference and track fraud in organizations prompting new detailed investigations
It plays a mega role in national defense, as it sifts thru videos with suspicious mentions
Judicial experts claim AI reduces bias in courts, resulting in recommended fairer sentences

Conscience-less robots have abilities to systematically form ideas that amass on the spot
If a nuclear code is acquired by them, it can make a decision that human groups may not
Which may be the result of a digital hallucinogenic error within a system of data overload
Protocols, mechanisms, and boundaries must be in place to gain a human trust mode

BIDEN'S APOLOGY

Colossians 3:13
Forgive as the Lord forgave you

The 1994 (Biden) Crime Bill was design to get tough on Crime in the United States
In 2022, President Joe Biden apologized for his part in shaping America's slate
Referred to as a Congressional Biden/Clinton Law Enforcement Act on Crime
Incentivized new prisons and created a <u>systematic</u> <u>mass</u> <u>incarceration</u> of all time

American increasingly complained about safety issues in the neighboring streets
Do something legislators, if you want to stay in those taxpayers' political seat
15 yr. minimums for non-violent drugs possession, 3 strikes were the contender
It was obsessive, and did not erase crime problems, or reduce repeat offenders

The most far-reaching negative impact was the <u>$12.5B</u> grant to build more jails
Incarceration rose <u>50%</u>, new facilities opened monthly, and the plight still failed
Black Caucus shared alternatives, jobs opportunities, and drug treatment plans
As stricter crime laws changed the trajectory of perhaps a once <u>hopeful</u> <u>man</u>

Most allotted funds were spent on new prisons with little left for trainings and or jobs
Implementation of the largest US crime bill failed, and communities again felt <u>robbed</u>
Pell grants were <u>eliminated</u> for those imprisoned when the 1994 Crime Bill passed
<u>No</u> formal education, abilities to obtain trades before inmate release, was the forecast

BIDEN'S BILLS PASSED

Matthew 5:37
Let what you say be simple, Yes or No, anything more than this comes from evil...

On 07/21/24, Pres. Biden dropped out of the race for president and endorsed his VP K. Harris
In this historical pivotal time if elected, she would be the 1st black female president leading us

#46 Pres. Joseph Biden started his term inside of a once in a century pandemic
Our world was forced into an emergency lockdown, real talk, no gimmicks
#46 used executive powers to pass 95 laws to reduce Americans constant delays
In contrast, #45 Trump managed 58 new laws +226 new judges with lifetime stays

In March 2021, a 1.9 trillion-dollar American Rescue Act became law of the land
It funded 2 stimulus checks and resources needed to implement Covid 19 plans
A Build Back Better goal was to create 1.5M jobs yearly w/equitable growth for all
Also attack the climate crisis w/ technical advancements to avoid irreversible falls

On 06/22/22, #46 made Juneteenth a federal holiday celebrating the freedom of blacks
It memorialized a 2 year wait of the 1865 Texas Law to end all the white slavery acts
In 2022, a Chips/Science Act was design to re-vitalize manufacturing in our states
Presenting a competitive US semi-conductor model to the world inside our gates

It provided access to high-speed internet and clean water in needed communities
#46 advocated successfully to lower high-cost drugs for persons with immunities
#46 coordinated successfully to get rid of junk fees added to purchases unfairly
A welcomed change for the working class whose budgets' success was "barely"

BIDEN and CLIMATE CONTROL

Genesis 8:22
While the earth remains, seedtime and harvest,
cold and heat, summer and winter, day and nights shall not cease

Climate data records provide evidence of climate change within key indicators
Rising sea levels, ice lost in glaciers, frequencies of severe weather stimulators
These factors are seen globally by the Nat'l Center for Environmental Info
Documenting new patterns developing more often, lasting longer shows

On the 1st UN address, #46 pledged to <u>double</u> amounts of int'l climate aide
This sparked a team approach to achieve more when plans were globally laid
Oil companies needed to reduce monies spent on <u>lobbying</u> to allow a change
And decide that it is <u>a duty to sustain our planet</u> with much to be rearrange

All the countries around the world would need to make this a <u>united</u> quest
Each <u>season,</u> new weather patterns present an urgency to act with zest
The science indicates this issue is at critical levels and is now here to stay
We will witness devastating results if we <u>ignore</u> what <u>will never go away</u>

Weather remains unstable with variations <u>persisting</u> for <u>longer periods of time</u>
It threatens future generations of weather stability is what science have defined
Greenhouse gas emissions are pushing the earth's temperature to higher degree
A large reduction of gas emission would reduce a lot of environmental <u>disease</u>

BIDEN AND CORPORATIONS

Psalms 37:21
The wicked borrows but does not pay back,
but the righteous is generous and gives

#46 disclosed <u>50 major corporations</u> where #45 found loopholes and <u>paid no taxes</u>
The rich benefitted by orchestrated legislation that was skewed and arrogantly relaxed
While the <u>working class</u> dutifully pay absorbent taxes, USA still purports us as a team
America's wealthiest is a mere 4% of the population obtained thru capitalistic schemes

#46 campaigned and made good on the things he made presidential promises on
Not 1, but <u>2 stimulus checks</u> were issued to most Americans' families to stay strong
Curtailed with ills in our states such as Covid, hurricanes, unemployment, and fires
<u>Simultaneously,</u> the priority was the <u>workers</u> to get back to work and be fully hired

#46 reported cost could potentially be "<u>0</u>", and the infrastructure <u>plan</u> could pay for itself
By raising tax revenues on the <u>rich</u> and granting a start to average working-class wealth
The cost was once <u>zero tax payment</u> on 8 trillion dollars' worth of businesses to the <u>rich</u>
US tax <u>payments</u> needed to be presented fairly and was legislated to implement a switch

As the wealthy gained thru investments and charitable donations to get huge write offs
The working class receive paychecks with <u>mandatory</u> deductions that #45 enacted as boss
Long Covid 19 lingered 12-14 weeks after onset, and created a wage loss of $2B per year
Healthcare cost, low productivity, working while ill, and <u>lives lost</u> were in very high gear

The '22 <u>Inflation Reduction Act</u> allotted $370B for climate controls and clean energies devices
This 10-yr. goal was to create shared prosperity to underserved communities to reduce crisis
<u>Building Back Better</u> with US supply chains will reduce debt and create jobs for the masses
Together everyone achieved more (TEAM) when combined resources and plans surpassed

BLACK LIVES MATTER (BLM)

Col. 1:16
All things were created by Him, for Him,
and in Him all things hold together...

Being a police officer is a tough job, Being Black is even tougher....

BLM is a political social movement that highlights racial inequalities experienced by blacks
Incidences of police brutality was verified by Secret Service and Park Police as charges stacked
BLM protest policies, laws, and unaccountability of murders got little to no justice to cite
Most cases used the "imminent danger" defense ignoring safer techniques or basic human rights

26M people left their homes during the pandemic to protest the murder of George Floyd
While in custody, white police forced a foot on his neck, as peers watched his life destroyed
26 y.o. Breonna Taylor was falsely shot to death due to a false no-knock warrant while in her bed
BLM demanded an investigation that revealed the warrant was bogus and incorrectly prepared

Fast forward George Floyd Justice and Policing Act was denied by a Senate vote in year 2021
Dems and the GOP couldn't agree, so it still sits with more delays to get it passed and done
The "qualified immunity" clause allows police to shoot, due to a threat or imminent danger
Is what repeatedly is justified in courts of Law, while police continue to kill black strangers

That 2020 killing of G. Floyd where an officer knee remained on his neck for 8 minutes
Sparked a protest within a global pandemic, displaying being pushed to the absolute limits
So, if our representatives continue to disregard all citizens' inclusive unalienable rights
The constitution will become mere words with no obtainments for blacks or their plight

Being a police officer is a tough job, Being Black is even tougher...

BLACKS AND VP HARRIS

Romans 2:11
For God shows no partiality

On 07/21/24, Pres. Biden dropped out of the race for president and endorsed his VP K. Harris
In this historical pivotal time if elected, she would be the 1st female black president leading us

After 3 yrs. in, stories were written about problems with VP Harris, and what does she do
How many stories were written about VP Pence, Biden, or Cheney for others to view
Everyone knows the focus stays on the Pres., Vices are ceremonial to always have #1's back
Many don't want her in that position, therefore created false narratives regarding a lack

V.P. Harris knows her position and is aware of her womanhood and that her skin color is black
As with Hillary Clinton, white men refused to believe informed women can make huge impacts
Israel, Pakistan, India, and Philippines are countries that have voted in females successful
As CA. Atty Gen., 2nd black US Senator, 1st Black VP, she's knows a VP would be stressful

As VP, Harris has signed over 285 tie-breaking bills into law, more than any VP before
Her vote on the Amer. Rescue Plan approved the stimulus checks that arrived at millions' door
She championed electric school buses, lead free water, and researched wildfires and droughts
In 2022, she attended 3 official events each day, totaling over 725 a yr. of duty she cranked out

On the centennial of the Tulsa Race Massacre, Biden created a federal inter-agency task force
VP Harris lead the investigation and found evidence of illegality activated as an entitled choice
It proved a systemic devaluation of homes of black & brown neighborhoods that was actively alive
PAVE (Property Appraisal and Valuation Equity) was a HUD inclusion for minorities to also thrive

Christina Trezevant McGriff

BLM: THE COLD WAR

Proverbs 27:17
"As Iron sharpens iron, so one person sharpens another"

Blacks watch 40 hrs. of TV weekly, more than any other race or time spent on a job
Algorithms dictate creativity that gained wealth thru clicks and actualities are robbed
We love Black Networks with visions of increased ownership within our own culture
Meanwhile, businesses watch high black consumer levels and capitalize like vultures

Sheila & Robert Johnson sold BET because viewership dropped and so did profit gain
They instead bought hotels/dealerships that employed blacks as growth was maintained
Cable bundled networks are becoming antiquated in households with a hit and major lost
We <u>must</u> unite to support black causes and independently seek to be our own best boss

Factual truth has power as people gravitate to the authenticity of any given story
When breaking news hit, most go to community experts for truth in all categories
An over saturation of features on beauty, fashion, sports, but little on money sense
As the new elections activates, lets create a design to support a <u>black news defense</u>

Termination, viewership, contributions, time, and the talents will get us there
The rich get richer off of innovative creations, then market to the masses aware
America is shifting with reversals, artificial intelligence, more guns to name a few
It is imperative to band together with ideas on how to universally navigate through

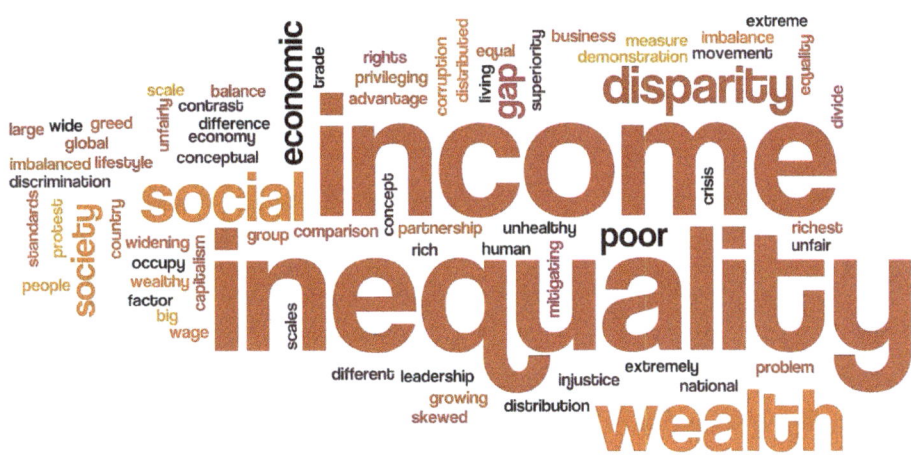

BORDER CONTROL

Deuteronomy 10:19
And you are to love those who are foreigners,
for you yourselves were foreigners in Egypt

Border control are measures taken by the government to monitor and regulate how things move
It includes people, animals, and goods travelling by land or air that are federally approved
US shares 7K mi. of borders, rivers, lakes and coastal waters with geo-restrictions prepared
In 2024, a bill was submitted to the GOPs to make the US-Mexican border safer and fair

In 2003, Custom Border Protection (CBP) created an agency focusing on integrity at ports of entry
Consolidation of responsibilities assisted in the compliance of trade laws and procedures intently
The goal to keep terrorist, weapons, and drugs out of the US + welcome travelers and commerce
The borders have made plans for an integrated approach so improvements will cont. to disperse

USA is known as a country who welcomes migrants for a chance of a safer prosperous life
Recent numbers of asylum seekers have stressed cities budgets causing an ongoing strife
Texas Gov. Abbott sent loads of migrants to cities without notice or time to create a plan
Arrived at safe cities by the 100's via planes, buses, trains seeking jobs and a better hand

Homeland Security mission was to stop fentanyl and other drugs from entering the USA
Two grains can be deadly, deaths #'s have increased 800% in 2 years is what the CDC say
Citizens are dying an est. of 1500 a day from drug traffic of international crime organizations
Borders are begging for more manpower to get better results with a vigor and determination

CITIZEN TRUMP

Exodus 20:16
You shall not bear false witness against your neighbors

45 is no longer a president; he is a <u>citizen</u> like the rest of us living in these United States
His <u>Make America Great Again</u> (Maga) supporters are enormous and always feel he's great
However, this self-absorbed, misogynistic person continues to dominate the news as a "victim"
Is allegedly the lead actor in the <u>Project 25</u> plan to change US <u>entire</u> landscape when stricken

Many uncharted territories evolved since the 45th presidency, with a swiftness to resolve
As a citizen, his antics have Dems and Gop's scurrying to be correct when getting involved
<u>91 cases and 6 indictments</u> has created a pattern of a person who <u>feels he is truly above the law</u>
Also being <u>twice</u> <u>impeached</u>, no conviction, showed law makers <u>inability</u> to discern what we saw

This lack of <u>governmental control</u> is hard to watch, as #45 show behaviors of wanting to be king
His art of gaslighting has prevented US progress with undemocratic ideas festering in the wings
Over <u>400 years</u> of privileges and <u>entitlements</u> are seen as automatic by some and always there
The <u>Browning of America by 2040,</u> will birth a new <u>majority race</u> the US census has declared

#45 is the first president to face charges in four states <u>simultaneously</u> while running for office
Georgia charged #45 and 19 others with RICO violations and falsifying info sent as authorized
He has <u>alleged</u> illegal kickbacks for national secrets, to foreign countries amounting to trillions
Increased national security threats has increased <u>US protections,</u> costing the US citizens billions

In NY., **<u>convicted</u>** for falsifying money records to S. Daniels to keep the 2016 votes afloat
In GA., charged with conspiring to overturn the 2020 election results with fraudulent votes
In FL., charged w/ mishandling WH docs, <u>dismissed by Judge Cannon and up for appeal</u>
In DC., with blocking an official proceeding via the <u>Jan. 6th insurrection</u>, all factually real

CLASSIFIED DOCUMENTS

Exodus 20:15
You shall not steal...

The DOJ requested #45 to return WH classified documents 3X to where they belong
The FBI then searched #45's home to recover said documents which made a criminal case strong
This tells the world that we have failed to control #45, who has no allegiance to his United States
These sensitive documents were found out in the open available for anyone to peruse and debate

#45 shoots himself in the foot with rhetoric surrounding his privileges and all his substantial deals
Such as groping women, and allowed to shoot anyone in broad daylight without the law at his heels
He's left Americans shaking their head about his since of responsibility, duty, and justice to all men
He was held accountable with appeals in place to be shielded from the "Rule of Law" once again

Delay tactics were created until after the vote so #45 could pardon himself and dismiss all charges
This intrusive act derails the focus of our American democracy, as the masses mistrust enlarges
NY lawsuits reported #45 fraudulently inflated the value of his property to get discounts in taxes
He was found criminal liable and paid $250M retribution, w/a 3 yr. pause on business transactions

Smith requested a Gag order to prevent harm to agents that #45 publicly repeats "wants him dead
Justice Cannon has been scrutinized for constant delays of critical trail dates needed to move ahead
AG Garland asked Counsel Smith to investigate the WH docs matter which yielded indictments
#45 plead not guilty, and a dismissal was granted from appointee Justice Cannon, with excitement

CLIMATE

Luke 21
And great earthquakes shall be in divers places, and famines, and pestilences and great signs shall there be from heaven.

Climatologists say the subject needs to be addressed <u>now</u> and placed in <u>front</u>
History shows revolutions start when folks <u>engage</u> a matter aimed to confront
Confront this alarming mounting issue that lingers towards the back seat
We need results now to prevent mega predicted disasters mounting to a defeat

90% of US companies are responsible for 75% of this <u>human</u> problem arising
<u>Nine million</u> people die yearly of verified toxic issues still actively comprising
Texas is categorized as the #1 area with the hottest winds stirring inside of the air
They had to demolish and rebuild an open stadium due to a <u>need</u> of A/C there

Decarbonizing energy has an ambitious 2035 year for a '0' vehicle emission goal
An active dense pollution called "<u>Black</u> <u>Snow</u>" at the borders remain uncontrolled
It settles dangerously inside of lungs, clothes, vehicles, or wherever it can stick
It's extremely costly to clean this sludge, hence plans to remove will not be quick

Biden met with leaders at the <u>Major Economic Forum on Energy and Climate</u> to discuss
How to globally team together on this time sensitive issue that has become a <u>must</u>
Expanding offshore wind opportunities in developing countries created progress and jobs
USA allocated the <u>most funds</u> towards a cleaner world to prevent lives from being robbed

Simultaneously II

CLIMATE CULTURE

Matthew 6:10
Jesus has both the wisdom and the power to prevent weather disasters

Agricultural and industrialized practices have increased greenhouse gas release
The result of the human release of pollutants has upset a once atmospheric ease
Wind, solar, and renewable energy sources would rid toxins and promote clean air
<u>Time is of the essence</u> as natural resources <u>erodes;</u> any action will show we <u>care</u>

2022 broke the record in the US for the hottest temperatures in 85 years to date
2023 Phoenix, Az. clocked an unbearable 105+ temps for an entire month straight
More extreme weather is expected scientifically to drop in and around our globe
We have been warned, we have been informed, hell-o <u>folks,</u> it's now being <u>disrobed</u>

<u>The Clean Air Act of 2022</u> says the EPA is responsible to protect the air in our space
It provided funding for new innovative technologies to mitigate new issues we face
#46 exec order promotes sustainability with carbon free electric and emission pollution
It diversified jobs around the US in an expected collaboration of resulting solutions

We all can make a difference with small changes applied to daily life everyday
Carpooling, electric vehicles, walking, or biking mitigates emissions in a <u>big</u> way
The World Global Forest serves as a lab to measure, observe, predicts and police
UN Educational, Science and Cultural Org. (NESCO) promotes a unified world peace

CODE RED (climate)

1 Corinthians 15:33
Do not be deceived: "Evil company corrupts good habits"

Climate is long-term temperatures received in a space over a period of time
Weather is short term temperatures received and can change on a dime
Hot and cold frequencies, intensities, storm waves, floods and the droughts
Has influenced new movements of weather patterns in our world throughout

Forecasters predicted and warned of new rapidly changing weather patterns
Illustrations of this destructive reality has been seen from the planet Saturn
Science shows the shifts remain hidden in the <u>caverns</u> until it <u>creates</u> a course
Hurricanes, tsunami, and tornados have now hit the world in a deadly force

Late night TV hosted multiple simulcast networks of talks about the urgency
U.S. is one of few nations who report climate on TV as an actual emergency
Droughts in Asia, Europe, S. America to the African rivers and in the valleys
Code Red, sound the alarm!!, for humanity to gather with lifesaving allies

The U.S. is at a <u>dangerous</u> crossroads of power where agendas get acquiesced to the top
It interacts globally with <u>controlling monopolies</u> of powers that are allowed to <u>swope</u>
It is reported to be <u>dark, underground, territorial, and conspiring</u> beyond any one's thought
If an insurrection on our capital can be <u>conducted,</u> what else is being secretly now sought?

CONSTITUTION (PART I)

Romans 13:8
Let no debt remain outstanding except the continuing debt
To love one another, for whoever loves others has fulfilled the law

"We the People" is the 1st words written in 1787 to the citizens of the United States

Judicial ancestors placed mechanism in place to protect our US Constitution
To prevent mischievousness of power and to instill joint lawful resolutions
Never in the history of the USA has divisiveness been so deliberately and overt
Sound the alarms fellow Americans, we are actively in stage "RED ALERT"!!

The insurrection on 01/06/21 showed how many Americans wanted to play ball
Separate the haves from the have nots, be damned thoughts of "Justice For All"
A mob of #45 supporters including ranking leaders stormed the capitol that day
To overturn the 2020 presidential election as citizens immediately began to pray

#45 threatened his own VP Pence's life with claims of him being at fault
Intel proved #45 directives was to invade, occupy, and by all means don't halt
As Justice Thomas's wife sent over 30 messages to #45 Chief advisor Meadows
The entire entanglement screamed an arrogant conspiracy that loudly bellowed

Congress is responsible for the planning of the judicial and executive branch sections
While the legislative branch creates and adjust laws as needed between elections
The Constitution has been amended only 27 times since 1797, most recently in 1992
The first 10 are the Bill of Rights as protection of free expression were pursued

CONSTITUTION (Part II)

John 11-35
Jesus Wept

Rep Liz Cheney denounced herself as a <u>republican</u> after the insurrection on Jan 6th
That violent crash into the capitol has been investigated and prayfully being fix
The Senate presents cult like characteristics that <u>ignored</u> most urgent needed task
Did we elect them to the office? or did they choose us to be <u>deceived</u> one might ask?

In 2018, #45 <u>disbanded</u> the WH pandemic response team along with all the funds
In 2019, with funds no longer available, Covid actions emergently needed to get done
National Security advisors pleaded to get a plan in place or devastation would be near
With no vaccine protections, the virus jumped to pandemic levels inciting a global fear

#45 questioned the cost of supplies such as masks and ventilators shipped to all states
#45 repeatedly publicly spewed <u>mis-information</u> as cases grew and failed to abate
#45 could have shut it down 3 months earlier when the intel was ominously <u>received</u>
His directive to America was "<u>it would magically go away</u>" and no need to take heed

The world <u>consequently</u> shut down with a mandatory quarantine to not go outside
It was very abrupt, immediate, and the <u>scientists</u> were the ones by which to abide
No living person had experience such a deadly situation that was scary to say the least
The world jumped into action and lost over 3M souls w/103M US cases to that beast

COVID CONTINUED

Psalms 91:3
Surely, He shall deliver you from the
snare of the fowler and from the perilous pestilence

In 1918, the Spanish Flu took over 675K lives with no vaccine developed to use
In 2023 close to 7M died with 700M confirmed cases is the number Covid19 abused
The symptoms mimicked sinusitis, allergies, congestion, bad colds and or the flu
It was hard to self-diagnosis but grew rapidly, with a need to know <u>exactly what to do</u>

Covid 19 carried many analytical discussions with countless endless debates
About the length of time took to develop and the need to publicly relate
Scientist monitored this virus for many years before and after the Covid threat
A major scientist who developed the vaccine is black, named **Kissmekia Corbett**

The (W.H.O.) reported 667M vaccines were administered in 2020 during that time
Employees were shown how to work from home, food workers were <u>not reassigned</u>
School age kids were given laptops and taught remotely by teachers made ready to go
Healthcare employees were <u>essential</u> in delivering people's need, and the <u>truest heroes</u>

For every (10) shots in the states, 3 were shipped to other countries as a need <u>met</u> in-kind
Biden administration shared more vaccines than over <u>100</u> other countries <u>combined</u>
500M shots to low-income countries and African received vaccines from the USA
Many stateside and global organizational teamed together and urgently jumped into play

In June '21 the new variant hit, the young got sicker faster as it lingered longer
Scientist returned into problem solving mode to help the infected get stronger
As the <u>Delta</u> variant was infecting kids in and out of schools at alarming rates
A lower adult dose was the final solution for the protection within the states

It settled in the respiratory tracks with some acute loss of smell and/or taste
The unvaccinated had no immunity to fight the beast with little time to waste
Vaccines were available for ages 12+, while younger shots were being approved
Pfizer granted an emergency use of the vaccine for the young as dosages moved

A major scientist who contributed to the development of the Covid 19 vaccine

Kissmekia Corbett

COVID PANDEMIC ENDS

Revelation 11:16
Seven angels will wield seven plagues in a
series of final severe judgements described in Revelations

The World Health Organization declared the end of the US Pandemic on <u>May 11, 2023</u>
It was a public health emergency of international concerns claiming 7M lives collectively
Thirteen million doses of vaccines were administered, and Europe had the highest rates
America fell in the middle while Africa had the least confirmed cases of death updates

Not one was excluded from contracting Covid 19 w/ deaths mounting every minute
It literally ceased movement everywhere, set humans down, with mandatory limits
The Covid 19 Pandemic came in like a tsunami taking breaths from anyone in its' path
It felt like <u>GOD</u> sent <u>a global warning</u> via a disease<u>, proclaiming disdain with a wrath</u>

The disease created a reflection time, goals changed, individually and collectively
A <u>great resignation</u> of jobs, priorities, and life goals were reconsidered respectfully
We learned that infectious disease controls needs <u>full funding</u> for a security of <u>health</u>
We learned masking up and social distancing worked when choosing to wear for <u>oneself</u>

Variants like Omicron and Delta created sub variances that happened down the line
Globally we now have a <u>genomic surveillance</u> of diseases to track better in <u>real time</u>
The risk is real, funding must be made a <u>priority</u>, we cannot set aside for later dates
Covid-19 Pandemic was a horrific experience that no living soul could ever underrate

CRITICAL RACE THEORY (CRT)

Malachi 2:10
"Do we not have one God? Did not one God create us"

Critical Race Theory is a cross-disciplinary movement of civil-rights scholars + progressives
Observed in the 80's, studies showed how courts gave leniency to some races as others regressed
This ingrained <u>white privilege</u> in the US has created <u>supremist hate groups</u> who always embrace
The minority numbers are <u>rising</u> while the majority population are declining within <u>their race</u>

Racism dates back to 1865 which manifested restrictions while other races got the nod
It rejected truth, evidence, or reasons to challenge ideas of an entire system being flawed
In 2020, white parents rallied not to teach about slavery to their kids who may get stressed
This white privilege is the result of who they have become, will we ever <u>address this mess?</u>

Critical thinking refers to a scholarly criticism of how and why we are in any said state
It reveals how social problems stem from social structures and not of an <u>individual's</u> fate
It argues that this <u>assumed</u> ideology is the largest <u>obstacles</u> blocking human liberation
Seeps into subsets, genders, ethnicity, and lawmaker's agendas w/ real transformations

It has a putrid smell of <u>inauthenticity</u> that demands to stay hidden and let's just forbid
Conservatives decided erasing <u>actual</u> <u>history</u> is again a <u>privilege</u> inside of <u>our U.S. grid</u>
Media, political, and social perceptions are valued by the masses as an imposed reality
As horrible injustices become desensitized into a normalcy that <u>remains</u> void of actualities

DEBT CEILING

Proverbs 22:7
The rich rules over the poor, and the borrower is the slave of the lender

In 2023, debt exceeded $33 trillion held by the public and other government accounts
Money borrowed to pay the nations' bills is a grave concern as debt steadily mounts
Like a home budget, national debt shows amounts due or left after paying yearly bills
When we borrow more than we can afford, US ratings drop with unpaid debt to fulfill

In 1945, we borrowed $75M from investors and the French to pay for war supplies
It enabled us to pay needed programs by law that constitutionally couldn't be denied
Americans are very concern as to why this debt continues to climb out of control
Lawmakers should stop bickering and make budgeting their only primary role

Yearly government shutdowns are threatened that effects citizens in the United States
If lawmakers' salaries were not guaranteed this behavior would not be in dire straits
We spend more than any other country on SSI, healthcare, and our national defense
Change the existing rules for successful results, and please, make it make sense

Any road repair cost may exceed the tax surplus on hand and start a budget decline
Focused concessions will need to be made post haste to keep US spending in line
US taxpayers employ the lawmakers to watch over our debt with a steady eye
We could see a surplus again, with engagements that yields winning hi-fives

DEMOCRACY

Acts 5:29
Then Peter and the other apostles answered and said,
We ought to obey God rather than men.

Our US Democratic system was united and admired around the global world
#45 rearranged that truth while participants engaged, and heads began to swirl
Half the nation experienced entitlements and disliked those not of their race
#45 said it out loud, followers disregarded the inequities in front your face

Unlawful bodies rehashed nasty racism stains that does not get addressed
Non-inclusiveness, and gerrymandering continues as key factors that depress
#45, Pres. Trump was the 1st ever to be impeached twice in one single term
Obstruction of Congress and Abuse of Power with no convictions affirmed

He mimicked an autocrat, and showed visuals of a power never seen before
Outlandish ideas and non-unifying speeches were divisive, and yet, not ignored
He's notorious for throwing others under a bus with untruths to lift his cause on any day
His perspectives benefitted only the rich while the have nots were ignored in every way

Black Lives Matter continued to rally and protest even while Covid-19 continued its' spread
More Blacks was getting murdered by white police officers with no accountabilities declared
The US was locked down via curfew and disease, not knowing who would live or die
#45 consistently diminished the emergency and lied, as an estimated 2.2M are now unalive

DOMESTIC VIOLENCE

Genesis: 6:11
The earth was also corrupt before
God and the earth was filled with <u>violence</u>

When eyes meet, you talk and can feel each other's vibe
You feel that tug in your heart that makes you glad to be alive
You then notice he/she doesn't want you to share your time with any others
You creep away from your normalcy, others notice, including your mother

Friends and families report you have a new "boo" and falling in-like
Then in-like and subtle changes grow and starts to eventually spike
You want to see how a good possibility can potentially turn out
Welcome the chase, an attentiveness, with <u>new</u> feelings of doubts

Domestic Violence and gaslighting crimes are higher than all others combined
Its prevalent around the world because relationships anywhere take time
Domestic Violence is alive and well and could be living somewhere near you
Stay in touch with your loved ones, to help in what <u>you</u> may be going through

Most things are not 100% at all times, everyone knows <u>intuitions</u> are real
Embrace it with mindful open arms, but scope out feelings of brewing deals
We go around once, <u>like</u> <u>may</u> turn into love, which remains an amazing thing
Listen to your heart, to be confident that <u>you're</u> <u>not</u> a target of a violent sting

ELECTORAL COLLEGE

Proverbs: 29:2
When the righteous thrive, the people rejoice, when the wicked rule,
the people groan

The electors meet every 4 yrs. to constitutionally formalize the new Pres and VP vote
Senators and representatives are not electors and do not assist in the matter or promote
The insurrection on Jan.6th was to block the vote, to not allow Biden in office via an attack
These extremists and supremist were provoked by Trump which resulted in a lot to unpack

The Insurrection on 01/06/21 remains the ugliest day witnessed by citizens scared straight
Over $30M in damages, deaths, suicides, and injuries was pushed by #45's ugly hate
In colonial days civil rights had no credence, only wig wearing men were allowed to lead
Some progress has now occurred extending rights to all genders, color, races and creeds

After the 2016 election, the U.S. was split on the antiquated electoral vote to keep or to toss
#45 won the presidency by 56% to Clinton 44% electoral votes is how he became the boss
Hillary Clinton won the national popular vote by 3M, and it has indeed happened before
A Popular only vote system would abolish an electoral process and this happening anymore

Let us learn from this catastrophe and not allow this to potentially ever happening again
The focus is to save our democracy by handling any obstacles and preparing only to win
Keep it simple with a single Win from a casted vote of your candidate of choice
Vacate the 2-tier electoral tradition, and any ideas of a devious insurrectional voice

ELECTORAL VOTE FOR 1892.

STATE.	VOTE.	REP.	DEM.	STATE.	VOTE.
Alabama	11			Montana	3
Arkansas	8			Nebraska	8
California	9			Nevada	3
Colorado	4			New Hampshire	4
Connecticut	6			New Jersey	10
Delaware	3			New York	36
Florida	4			North Carolina	11
Georgia	13			North Dakota	3
Idaho	3			Ohio	23
Illinois	24			Oregon	4
Indiana	15			Pennsylvania	32

FULLY VACCINATED

Philippians 2:4
Let each of you look out not only for
your own interest, but also, for the interest of others

Coordinating to receive the Covid vaccine was an individual choice decided by self
A controversial personalized decision, effected the masses and everyone's health
Not mandatory, but developed by a black female scientist who mitigated the spread
The virus mutated around the world with **7 million** living souls pronounced dead

Creative incentives by #46 to take the vaccine were immediately put into place
The death toll rose exponentially as the <u>world</u> participated in this race
Vaccines were given <u>freely to all citizens</u> who followed the science and agreed
Convenient locations were placed and utilized, to slow the virus from running free

Three fourths of Americans are now fully vaccinated is what the data say
However, the <u>70M</u> <u>unvaccinated</u> Americans increase a health risk everyday
Everyone had friends or family members with unwavering opinions or thoughts
The goal was to reduce the severity of <u>hospitalizations</u> the Covid virus brought

After the second variant <u>Omicron</u> reared its aggressive ugly head
Cases increased even more rapidly as well as the number of persons dead
President Biden had <u>4 free test kits</u> shipped to every <u>household</u> who applied
Also, <u>N95 mask</u> were available free to Americans via a government supply

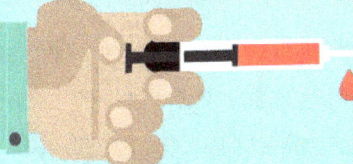

GLOBALIZATION

Colossians 3:3
Set your minds on things that are above and not on things on earth

Globalization has had a fast-changing effect on traditional cultures and ideas
Who feels our way of life is now being challenged with concerns causing fears
Mass killings by guns are reported increasing each day with little change in sight
While citizens <u>beg</u> legislators to change the rules to reduce an unnecessary plight

Democracy aims to embrace enrichments of cultures even when <u>they</u> don't agree
Two countries Kuwait vs Russia, and Israel vs Gaza are <u>at war</u> fighting to be free
From unresolved issues that has caused sneak attacks via air, land, and the sea
Thousands are dead, and more injured while seeking safety and a place to flee

These wars are lengthy and cost millions borrowed, or granted by allies of states
Policies and procedures evolve daily to anticipate how and when to retaliate
These countries seek aid and weapons from China and the USA to assist in a win
Strategic talks got intense, purposing not to spread aggression into a <u>global</u> spin

Global governance entails political cooperation among the transnational actors
It aims to resolve disputes and enforce rules while analyzing multiple factors
The United Nation sets in an <u>advisory role only</u>, surrounding diplomatic relations
Technology and/or trade incentives has increased these political eco-globalization

GLOBAL INNOVATIONS

Psalms 19:1
The heavens declare the glory of God,
and the sky above proclaims his handiwork

In 1962, #35 JFK, dared the world to think <u>Moon-Shot</u> w/a man on the moon in 10 years
Now, new contestants submitted inventions for a $1M prize award with exceptional ideas
In 2022, JFK was honored in Boston where the 3rd <u>Earth Shot</u> award winner was revealed
Prince Wm. of the BBC transferred that shot to **"save the planet"** as the needed appeal

Excited global nominees had concepts and solutions discussed in detail
How to build and re-imagine issues that Earth urgently needs to curtail
To sustain a <u>Waste Free World</u> is up to <u>humans</u> to systematically get to yes
300M global pounds of waste a year is a concern that destroys earths' progress

Winners will <u>focus ten years</u> on nature, waste, climate, and clean air sparing no time
Honorable mentions on the list below displays incoming talent that has a bright shine
Kenya: 200K natives used a clean stove invention which saved $10M in fuel cost and care
India: Greenhouse in a Box protects farmers and adds growth thru plastic in frosted air

UK: <u>Grand Prize Winners</u> developed an alternative to plastic thru plants and seaweed
With biodegradable packaging that holds liquids w/ an elimination of waste guaranteed
Oman: Removal of CO_2 could reduce global warming by mineralizing the Peridotite rock
A new mineralization process of pumping carbonated water into the stones that interlock

A <u>2030</u> goal is to have a physical colony on the moon represented by the USA
If the <u>2024</u> space mission is successful, the goal becomes do-able and not very far away
We are not alone in this universe and curiosity satisfies our thirst to measurably know
Only then, will we expand the facts, learn more, and successfully exponentially grow

GREAT RESIGNATION

In the US. We tend to equate staying and stability with blessing and success. But God can work through uncertainty and disruption as well

As the uninvited Covid 19 brought the world to a three-year sudden shut down
Globally, 676 million were infected with over 3M <u>deaths</u> across our <u>US</u> towns
Staying inside was a must while repositioning activities was a strategized need
Cooperation was mandatory and a "Plan B" was always made in focused speed

Meanwhile, 47M dissatisfied workers <u>voluntarily</u> quit their jobs without any tears
Mostly Gen Z's and grads were ready to marry, and start a family worthy career
The concerns were education, economy, quality engagements and their mental health
Resulted in a deep reflection that transformed a meaning of what is <u>true wealth</u>

This brought an increased deficit of employees in an already stressed labor force
Incentives were created to get new hires and help companies to stay on course
The restaurant businesses took a <u>massive</u> fall due to customers not eating out
Well-known businesses sadly threw in the towel to what they once were about

The Labor Force is still dealing with an inadequate number of workers on board
They preferred an independent entrepreneurship was what they now explored
For millions to choose this path makes <u>statements</u> about our workers of today
Fair living wages, flexible hours, and reasonable work protocols is the prudent way

GUN VIOLENCE 1

Ecclesiastes 9:18
Wisdom is better than weapon of wars;
but one sinner destroyed much good.

Gun violence is still rampant with senseless deaths throughout cities in the US
Hospitals reported more young die from guns than car accidents in this mess
Conversation, proposals, and new strategies were put into lowering the numbers
Death rates still rose, and victims are reported as getting younger and <u>younger</u>

<u>Guns, guns, and</u> more <u>guns</u> is the major issue in the US by <u>lawmakers' design</u>
Research shows the US have more guns than <u>all other countries</u> combined
Locals manufacture guns from <u>3D machines</u> with no <u>ID numbers</u> to track
Repeated crimes stay unresolved, and police plead for help as cases <u>stack</u>

A six y.o. brought a gun to school and shot his 1st grade teacher was indeed real
Meanwhile, an 18 y.o. sold a puppy to a buyer who offered a <u>gun</u> to seal the deal
Perhaps MD <u>1st Black Gov. Moore</u> will create a plan other community will imitate
<u>Immediate</u> revised gun laws are the <u>only</u> decision that will reduce deaths in our states

Exposure to guns as a child increases trauma in an environment that effects the brain
Safety precautions, non-violent programs, and toys, help children get properly trained
The most <u>effective</u> violence prevention includes parents and family educational programs
Public policies and therapeutic interventions also reduce risk factors that prevent scams

GUN VIOLENCE II

Corinthians 10:4
For the weapons of our warfare are not of the flesh,
but has divine power to destroy strongholds

Devastation across the US states have death by guns in <u>epidemic</u> high rates
US lawmakers has failed to control the influx of guns presence is no mistake
There are more guns in <u>this country</u> than any other country on the planet earth
Other countries have systems in place, protecting their citizens' <u>value and worth</u>

Unnecessary funerals were prepared for massive numbers of precious human life
Our legislators ignore the repeated purchasing of guns that has escalated the strife
Citizens are requesting legal accountabilities and punishments across the US states
The US is <u>out of control</u> in our streets, schools, and churches when they spew hate

The outrage has a <u>haunting</u> pain as our justice system does not act on our pleas
As taxpayers want <u>new laws</u> created urgently, why don't they agree?
Congress can vote the <u>elimination</u> of <u>gun manufacturers</u>, and <u>protective immunity</u>
Increase background checks, safe storages, and health services into our communities

Statistics show deaths are from <u>assault weapons</u> of citizens under the age of twenty-two
The National Rifle Assoc. pay lobbyist and tote babies to conventions whose lives are new
It's a <u>US epidemic</u>, <u>a public health emergency</u>, denying citizens of their protective rights
With no actionable resolve, a <u>divine intervention</u> would help communities win this fight

HAITI

Proverbs 13:20
He who walks with wise men will be wise,
But the companion of fools will suffer harm

Over 12K Haitians piled into the US-Mexican borders in hopes to get out safe
To escape corruption, political instability, and natural disasters as of late
They were unaccepted and patrolled by horses handling them like cattle
The world observed this insensitivity in disbelief, and still remain rattled

The dictatorship country has always endured poverty and political instability
In 2021, 20K migrants trekked 60-mi. of dangerous jungles to escape humility
They fled their country out of total desperation seeking asylum in our USA
Families finally arrived unwelcomed, and people of color was turned away

Armed gangs savagely took control of the fuel source making the citizens weak
Deemed as an internal civil war, 1M+ Haitians have no water or food to eat
The gangs took over governance where only 3 out of 12 justices worked by force
The gangs used retaliation as a weapon, while citizens have no recourse

As of 2022, Haitian prisons held over 3X the detainees that it was structured for
With deplorable condition, violence, and malnutritional deaths were at the exit door
Year 2024. is scheduled to resume court hearings allowing time for the country reset
Haiti is also part of our world, let's not treat them as "a country we want to forget"

 HAPPINESS

John 16:4
Until now you have asked nothing in My name...
Ask and you shall receive, that you may be full

Happiness is purposefully created inside with added family and friends
Unlimited paths of joy fill the quiet spaces and take control for a win
After Covid-19, mental health problems escalated with multiple issues to address
As the world turned, a search for a steady mindset was a daily goal and test

Enjoy God's natural rainbows and the seasons given to us for free
Embrace friends and families' gatherings as they smile with glee
Enjoy the laughter of comedy that lightens up the dark spots in life
Play your favorite music that melts the worry inside and releases strife

Feelings at times you need a pause to process situations that make you think
Warning! over thinking can be dangerous, exercise can become a better link
Know your regularly choices of foods effects your mind, body, and your soul
Increase water, fruits/nuts, and vegetables, and reduce meats within your control

Seeking therapy to understand thoughts displays a respectful act to <u>self</u>
<u>Only you</u> can activate this process to quiet the demons, not <u>anyone</u> else!!
Be your own best friend, investigate the process and give it a <u>go and try</u>
To know that you know, <u>you</u> engage a process that may help clarify

Let's become our own best friend and do better as precious time past
You may surprise yourself and find a peaceful lifestyle that last
Your mental health drives who, what, when and how you become you
Do it, <u>chief executive officer (CEO),</u> and give yourself what you're due

IMMIGRATION

Exodus 22:21
Do not mistreat or oppress foreigners in Egypt

Immigration is the source of a population growth with cultural changes throughout
US has the highest number of immigrant movement in the world without a doubt
As of 2019, out of 244M, over 50M are in the US at a 15% growth rate assessed
Trump used executive orders that increased deportation by 45% with new arrest

Title 42 activation during Covid halted immigrants from crossing the borders
Migration ceased, to prevent the contagious Covid spread was the new order
Border control returned immigrants to facilities where the virus could transmit
Biden wanted to lift Title 42, return to Title 8 by processing data and submit

Transportation was arranged by the US for some to return and some did remain
NY, MA and MD have a Right to Shelter fund for them to enter our domain
The numbers are now out of control and putting strains on most cities in the USA
The need for food, housing, and schooling amplifies multiple problems each day

The new immigrants have no family connections here as they once had in the past
Instead of individuals, entire families, are crossing borders for a future to amass
Migrants use to spread quietly, organically, and gradually cross into the US states
According to Republicans, they now arrive in groups of chaotic bus loads as of late

IMMUNITY

John 10:10
The thief comes only to <u>steal and kill and destroy</u>
I came that they may have life and have it abundantly

As the 2024 elections continued, Counsel Smith pose the question to Scotus regarding immunity
<u>Is a 2x impeached</u> <u>ex-pres. w/a conviction</u> eligible to <u>run for President again</u> in our communities
#45 was recently <u>convicted</u>, with <u>5</u> indictments and <u>90</u> charges in <u>four</u> different separate states
Brought the founders' implementation of the Constitution's "<u>Rules of Law,</u>" into deep debates

6 conservatives (for) & 3 liberals (against) Justices, ruled on how <u>exactly</u> this issue will go
After over 100 days, <u>Scotus</u> ruled on <u>full immunity in any official</u> setting was the new <u>show</u>
Scotus decided a president could give <u>any directive</u> with no accountabilities was a lot to unpack
Proof of <u>non-official acts</u> would need to be decided <u>only</u> by the <u>Scotus,</u> to declare an actual <u>fact</u>

Founders divided the Federal Government into 3 branches to <u>check and balance</u> all in the team
Legislators makes the Laws, Executive carries it out, and Judicial interprets, void of any schemes
This was created to ensure the <u>protection of citizens' rights</u> through each branch of responsibility
It ensured one branch didn't <u>overpower another</u>, with mechanisms that activated an enforceability

Never in the history of American has a <u>SCOTUS</u> ruled with such disregard for our democracy
These <u>lifetime</u> <u>appointees</u> knew exactly what was at stake, and accepted #45 plan of autocracy
It showed righteousness met nothing, and <u>emboldened selfish ambitions is now the new mission</u>
The election will decide if democracy will stand, or if the <u>USA</u> will <u>change</u> beyond all recognition

Trump's multiple cases will get re-scheduled to be heard after the presidential Nov. elections
If he wins, #45 plans to <u>pardon himself</u> and create his self-absorbed dictatorship perception
AG Garland, remained adamant about the <u>Rule of Law</u> for everyone with no exceptions
However, many questioned his <u>delay</u> in officially charging #45, after he lost the <u>2020</u> election

86th Attorney General, Merrick Garland

INCLUSIVITY

Proverbs 27:17
As iron sharpens iron, so does one person sharpen another

A $42B program was released to close a digital divide in residences unable to pay the rates
A $426B Infrastructure Bill made improvements to outside structures around US states
These hefty funds passed by Congress, created jobs and increased pay for the working class
Willing citizens are excited about job opportunities, as decent salaries will finally amass

#46 successful reduction of monthly Rx cost dramatically help citizens' budgets reduce
Teamwork at the federal/state levels allowed Pharma to cost effectively mass produce
Interventions in healthcare, nutrition, housing, and education simultaneously helped more
Inclusiveness for all, end exclusiveness of the entitled, where things never stood before

Reparation is the least the US can give Blacks who was declared 3/5th of 1, and denied a vote
It systematically enslaved, stripped dreams and opportunities of a future that is still afloat
The Geoge Floyd Act would create DOJ investigations and accountabilities of wrongful acts
The Senate would need to address each matter with real evidence and only authentic facts

As we continue a fast-paced life of distractions and reactions, keep our eyes on father time
Witnessing a failed insurrection that wanted to destroy democracy was a heinous crime
As #45 thanked Blacks publicly, for not voting when he won the election in year 2016
This 2X impeached criminal wants vengeance in America, and says exactly what he means

INDICTMENTS OF #45

Isaiah 5:23
Who acquit the guilty for a bribe and deprive the innocence of his right

Trump has been indicted by the FBI 4 times for criminal charges against his own USA
He was the 1st president investigated and charged by his own cabinet officials in dismay
Three conspiracies were reported as facts, as defendant #45 disputed them everyday
His lies were criminally laced, governing was not his concern, only how he played

Special council Jack Smith also listed how #45 prevented US citizens a right to vote
In as many as seven states, he fraudulently and unlawful undermined law with a bloat
He allegedly exploited the violence on Jan. 6 and sought means to seek and destroy
The world watched the dilemma in disbelief, as security was suspiciously ignored

The 01/06/21 insurrection became the largest investigation in the history of the USA
Obstruction of an official procedures with 6 co-conspirators is in court until verdict day
A reduced amount of police defended the capitol and was the heroes in all ways
As Vice President Pence testified to the DOJ about his refusal to accept #45 melee

The White majority has decreased in population with a verifiable non-white growth
A fear of losing entitlements has created a group behavior commitment to their oath
#45 continued to campaign for presidency always with his cult-like mounting support
His schedules remained limited, due to his mandatory presence in multiple courts

INFRASTRUCTURE

Exodus 27:1
And you shall make the alter of acacia wood, five cubits long and
Five cubits wide; the alter shall be square and its height shall be three cubits

Like we care for homes inside, outside infrastructures needs care as time passes by
In Nov '21, Biden signed a <u>trillion-dollar</u> <u>Infrastructure Bill</u> under many watchful eyes
Billions went into state/local upgrades of bridges, water, transits systems, and roads
It was #46 largest <u>bipartisan</u> win that gave taxpayers hope to obtain more control

#46 wanted lawmakers to focus less on wants and more on what could get <u>passed</u>
Build, Back, Better was his mantra that identified ambitious goals that were vast
Our taxes pay the lawmakers to allocate funds and repair communities and states
This gives citizens solace to know that their cargo and travel sites will remain safe

This <u>historic</u> <u>win</u> will repair parts of America not considered in over forty years
It will expand clean water and high-speed internet access to locations that are dear
Its' goal is to invest in communities that has too often been left out of inclusivity
Good union paying jobs sustains the economy for <u>all</u> to embrace an attainability

The Bill will build a US network of electric vehicle chargers and create local jobs
Updated infrastructure will deliver clean energy technology, to reduce emission clogs
A $50M weatherization package was granted for products that reduces floods and fires
America will witness massive infrastructure maintenance that will yield ready new hires

INSURRECTION

Ezra 4:19
I decreed, a search has been made, and it has been found that this city of old time has made an insurrection against kings, rebellion and sedition have been made therein

We have reached the 3rd anniversary of the 01/06/21 attack on our nations' capitol
One defendant's permission to go out of the county was deemed not apropos
This domestic attack on democracy was <u>the</u> most heinous act America have ever seen
The deliberate planning and willingness to <u>execute</u> was a volatile destructive <u>scheme</u>

While the world was <u>simultaneously</u> addressing the deadly virus named Covid-19
#45 Donald Trump, went on live TV and insighted an unforgettable scene
#45 could not accept, after appeals, that he was ineligible to run for a 2nd term
Unprecedented numbers came out <u>against</u> this presidency is what he learned

"Storm the Swamp" was the directive from #45 to his willing loyal followers
A display of terrorism within our own country as <u>all</u> screamed and <u>all</u> hollered
They purposefully stormed the capitol to attack and caused much undue mayhem
His VP Pence had the authority to certify the vote, was also on the list to <u>condemn</u>

#45 remained loyal to him alone, America has never witnessed such a disgusting sight
Police manpower was suspiciously low, help arrived hours later, despite what was right
A commission was formed, to discuss how exactly was this allowed a <u>green light</u>
<u>Leaders</u> purposely failed to protect the capitol and staff, once #45 <u>plans</u> took flight

MAGA

Psalms 52:2
Your tongue devises destructions like a sharp razor, O worker of deceit

MAGA is a slogan repeated by #45 during his Pres. campaign backed by supporters
This phenomenon was explained by scholars as dog whistles of coded scripts and orders
It proclaims the states can manage and encourage enterprise for all America to succeed
#45 obtained opened doors backed by his presidency with a monumental selfish greed

According to a U of WA study, the minds of Maga supporters revealed hatred of Blacks
They see their population decreasing and being replaced by minorities and feel the lack
This attitude penetrated the GOP lawmakers that halted focus of any work getting done
Postering, ego stroking, majoring on the minor and of course, the presidential re-run

They believe in pro-life, gun, police rights, and believe the re-election was stolen
This canvass divided values systems that had been infiltrated and swollen
The group believes #45 can create a 1950's style white majority with benefits
Data show mixed races has created a browning which became his newest nemesis

#45 psychologically duped 1/2 of America that he can sustain benefits for all whites
Blinded by his misogynistic behaviors and illegal acts, he disregarded what was right
He announced his VP pick JD Vance, a 39-year-old republican senator from Ohio
Married to an Indian attorney, 2 kids, and chummy with Donald Jr. is all we know

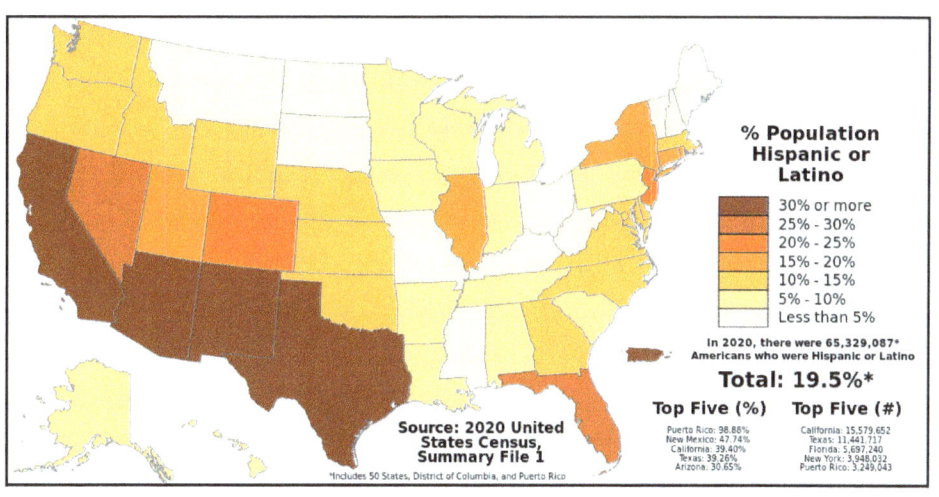

MENTAL HEALTH

John 1-9:
If we confess our sins, he is faithful and just to forgive us,
our sins, and to cleanse us from all unrighteousness

Mental disorders are impairments of the mind causing distress of personal functioning
It stems from childhood traumas, addictions, or feelings of isolation at any junction
Causes are complex and varies depending on the individual's diagnosis
Assessments and treatment can provide safe spaces to heal from specific prognosis

The world is currently facing an inordinate spike of mental health stress
As we transverse daily tasks, things in moderation becomes the true test
When things overwhelm, take a day to reset to a pace that's good for you
Plan realistically what new days will look like, and what you need to do

An ability to cope, adjust, and adapt is key for clarity and peace of mind
Families experienced anxieties with limited abilities to reflect and redesign
Working from home, disruptions, and multitasking the list of things to complete
Do things for that day only and allow the rest to be placed on tomorrow's seat

The stigma employs a hesitation not to say anything to relatives or friends
Find someone you trust to occasionally talk about things, and not pretend
An objective balanced trusted friend or counselor is a safe place to start
Reduce social medias, and replace with self-care habits to set you apart

MOON TRIPS

Psalm 148:3
Praise him sun and moon, Praise him all the stars of light!

The moon is the closest to Earth in our universe and explored all the time
Luna, launched by Russia, had the 1st physical surface contact in 1959
Prior to that, the only means was thru observation and data sources from Earth
Now, over 150 missions have launched w/humans and robots gaining worth

Billionaires now create their own journeys to the moon who are not astronauts
That's what money does when creating a plan, is to finance their own shots
It's amazing how far US technology has advanced in space travel
Plans with backers adds answer to questions that get more info unraveled

The moon remains a popular target and a major destination for us
The first trip in Aug 2020 was a 15-minute Florida blast off gust
It was a huge success as the world watched in awe and wonder
A trip in Sept. will host 8 specially chosen citizens in that number

Nasa is preparing to send humans back to the moon in the Artemis Program
As of Sept'23, 29 countries have signed plans to create a space grand slam
Artemis 2 is planning a trip around the moon with a crew of four in 2024
Artemis 3 is planning a landing on the moon's South Pole in 2025, and more

Christina Trezevant McGriff

9/11/2001 (911)

Peter1 3:14
And if you suffer for righteousness' sake, happy
are ye, and be not afraid of their terror, neither be troubled

09/11/2021 hit the 20-year mark of terrorist bombings on US soil
In reflections are we safer now? opposite opinions continue to toil
A 9-11 memorial was erected capturing the devastation of that day
America families wanted a place to reflect when needing to get away

4 Islamic suicide terrorist attacks were carried out by al-Qaeda spewing hate for the USA
19 terrorists hijacked 4 commercial airlines crashing 2 into the NY Twin Towers that day
A 3rd crashed into the Va. Pentagon, and a $4^{th\,was}$ hijacked by passengers landing in PA
Over 3K lives were lost that day from a strategized attacks of martyr displays

The attack was unexpectedly gruesome and devastated Americans respectively
343 heroic firefighters ran into burning buildings and saved lives aggressively
To date, 257 died from the toxins alone that continuously hovered in the air
Organizations raised money and awareness to support families and cared

The extremist saw the US as obstacles, preventing Islamics from reaching global destinies
They believed violence as needed, to get Gods final revelation in the Qur'an as heavenly
Cancer, mental illness, survival guilt, and PTSD lead the list of what survivors shared
The humanity and heroism in the aftermath, displayed how much citizens cared

OPIATES

Ephesians 5:18
Do not get drunk on wine which leads to debauchery,
Instead, be filled with the Spirit

Drug overdose both fatal and non-fatal continues to plaque USA soil
The deaths come from synthetic opiates and by manufactured fentanyl
The DEA has confiscated over 50 million deadly laced pills
Internet sales of counterfeit drugs has dominated the societal ills

A 350% increase from Mexico was enough to kill every person in the USA
Combined with illicit drugs sold to investors produced dangerous patterns today
Teens between 12 to 18 are vulnerable with peer groups that spreads the word
As to what, when, and where they can obtain drugs and how it gets transferred

The CDC (Center for Disease Control) has raised public awareness for all to discuss
Quickly street drugs and prescription opiates become addictive and will self-destruct
It destroys families. and productive healthy relationships break down to new lows
Reach out and embrace the tested resources to increase what you actually know

We must come together with all of our minds and with all of our might
To create safe pain treatments, when researching and development unites
US and China brokered a deal to halt exports to Mexico headed to the USA
Those negotiations reduced overdosing deaths, occurring in cities everyday

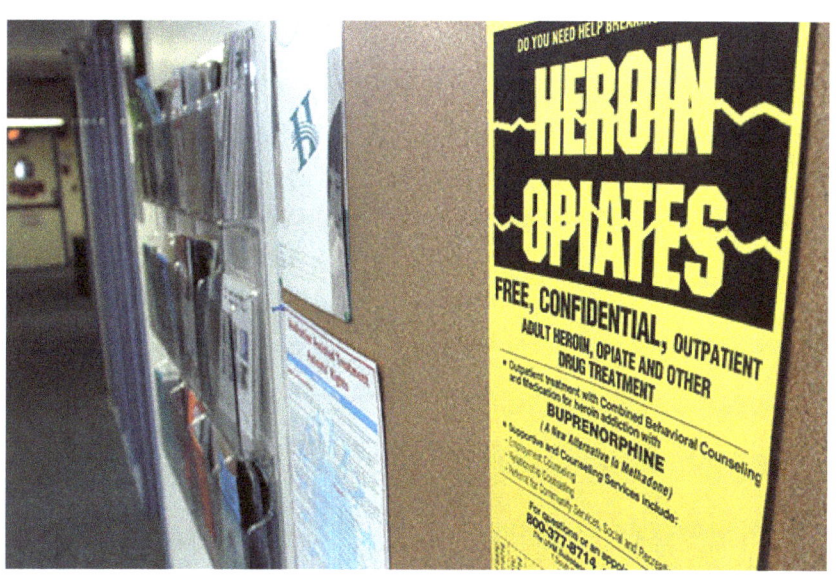

POLICE REFORM

Proverbs 21:15
When justice is done, it is a joy to the righteous but terror to evildoers

George Floyd Police Reform Act was shot down in the Senate in Sept. 2021
Reason being the "qualified immunity" clause delayed things from getting done
It protected deaths caused by police due to "feeling threatened" and had to shoot
Disproportionate numbers of unarmed blacks are dead in defense of that pursuit

Citizens remain disappointed that legislators have not prioritized the need to act
Even the publicized murder of G. Floyd did not give credence to apparent facts
Police depts. implemented de-escalating techniques to use in streets across states
This was a band aid tactic, as only new laws will reduce victims due to hate

Public unrest hit a high after the murder of B. Taylor and G. Floyd in 2020
A national protest proliferated in support of Black Lives Matter gathered plenty
A reallocation of funds from policing to services was on the table to make a change
A new framed behavior of listening granted dignity for things to possibly re-arranged

Retirements and resignations rose due to an inability to embrace a need for change
Communication and relationships within the police department became estranged
Citizens still see policemen as a threat, not as the proverbial protect and serve
Community trauma informed services is what citizens want and lawfully deserve

ROE VS WADE 1

A right to choose...

This unmarried woman did not want a 3rd child, while struggling with the existing 2 Abortion laws were made by men, who will never experience what women go through

In 1973, a pregnant woman of 2 challenged her right to have another child or not
It resulted in a debate granting a <u>landmark</u> decision for women, and <u>was indeed a lot</u>
It eliminated underground abortions that caused medical issues and many deaths
It allowed women to choose if a birth was prudent, or if an abortion would be best

Since the 1800's, ethical and legal debates were ruled by <u>men</u> within a bias debate
Women weren't included into decisions, creating sexism and racism issues on plates
In Dallas TX, it went to court, her name was changed to *Roe* to protect her cause
She complained the laws didn't honor the US amendments, which gave her pause

Supreme Justices in '21 overturned the '73 law to <u>abortions</u> <u>now</u> seen as a crimes
It brought chaos and legal battles, that's <u>simultaneously</u> being unpacked in real time
63% of Americans didn't want the law overturned resulting in new imposed restrictions
In 2022, Scotus overturned abortion and left states to amend <u>their</u> renewed convictions

Norma McCorvey was a real person who sued the state b/c she was denied an abortion
She was a mother who <u>chose not</u> to carry her pregnancy to term with mindful precautions
She had birthed 2 babies that was given up for adoption and requested her due process
She felt the laws didn't protect her reasons, and men disrespected her & understood less

Scotus reversed *Roe vs Wade* decision after 50 years, declaring abortion unconstitutional
However individual states were granted a right to decide if the procedure was excusable
Consequently, today's youth will age with <u>fewer</u> <u>rights</u> than their mothers observed
A situation now governed by law, with an increased cost to the mother undeserved

Since the decision, patient's care and safety has been enforced thru penalties and jailtime
Some states have bounty hunters seeking female lawbreakers for these specified crime
It affected marginalized groups within race, income, and health accessibilities
In addition to travel cost to clinics out of state, added to the lack of possibilities

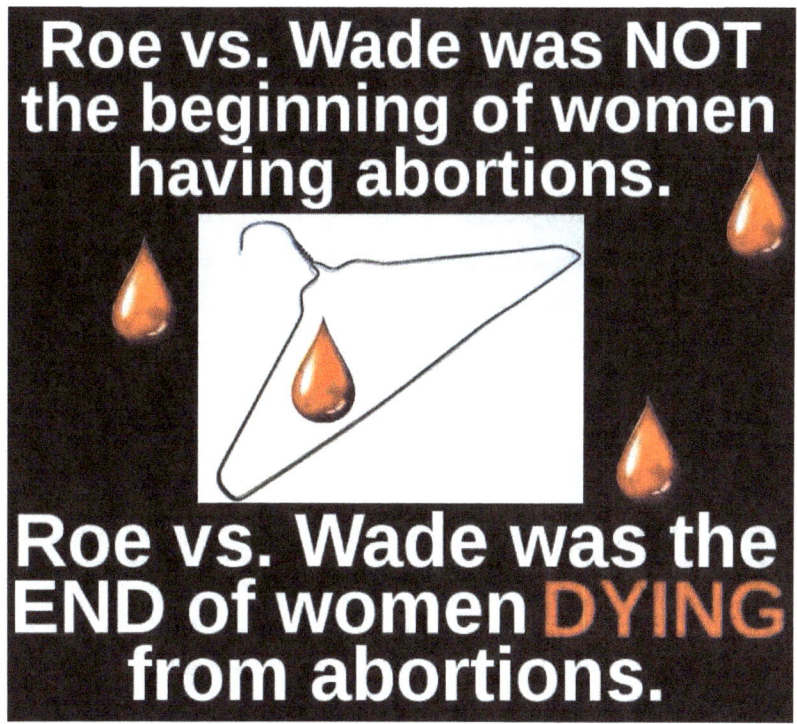

SCOTUS AND VACCINES

Proverbs 3: 4-5
We are free to make any choice, but we are not free to
exempt ourselves from the consequences of those choices!

Vaccine mandates and protocols changed every day which caused a national divide
One thing was certain the Omicron variant was aggressive, and no one could hide
Biden requested all Federal workers to be vaccinated or get a weekly test
Attorneys took it to the Supreme Court who allegedly, failed to do their best

They were established to solve pressing issues and discuss the lawful words
The "Equal Justice Under the Law" responsibility was to allow all to be heard
Appointed justices ruled on vaccine mandates, with no opinions or legalities built in
Biden's directive for 12M federal workers to get shots cancelled, If not now, <u>WHEN</u>

The 3rd year into this viral global pandemic scientists scurried to reduce the spread
The <u>spirit of the law</u> was <u>not</u> considered, as 700K victims were <u>now dead</u>
Rising infections soared to over 2 million globally as it remained harder to control
The Scotus sided with individual rights as deaths mounted their lifeless souls

Even with uncertainty, destruction, and corruption, Jesus will remain great
With ongoing stress, the impossible remained possible, when one avoided hate
Our God was at his breaking point, yet still lifted his children to restore peace
His promises <u>remained</u> <u>guaranteed</u> to those who <u>believed,</u> in the mist of disease

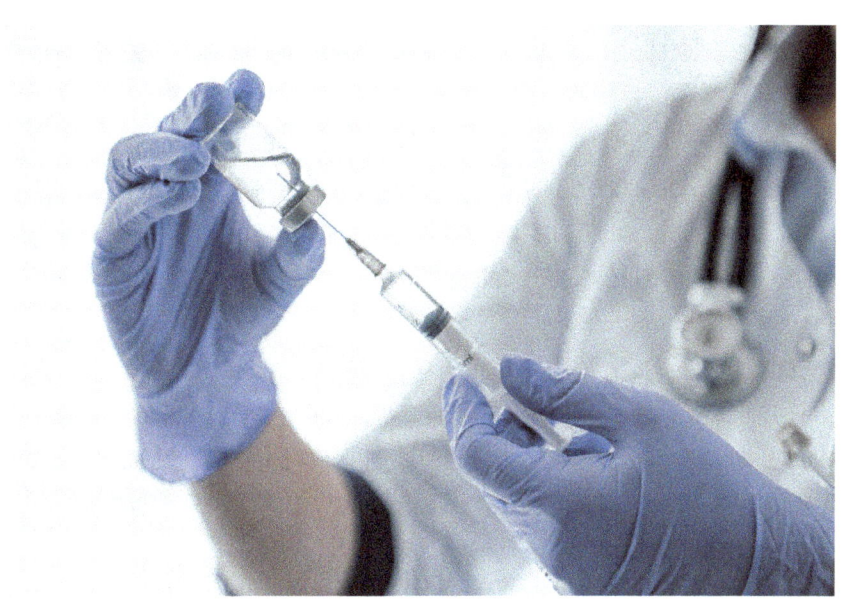

STATE OF THE UNION

A yearly address delivered each January by the president of the United States to a joint session of the US Congress, discussing the current state of our nation

In 2023, 46th President Biden delivered his 2nd state of the union to citizens of the US
Seeking the 118th Congressional bipartisanship on needed improvements we face
Retired, Speaker Pelosi present as the 1st <u>women</u> to lead the Dems Party for over 20 years
Hakeem Jeffries present as <u>1st Black House Minority leader</u>, unanimously elected by peers

#46 focused on local America plans to Build Back Better from bottom up to middle out
An importance of USA made products that sustains workers in <u>our</u> country throughout
Build Back Better historic Infrastructure Act 2022, budget is 1.2T gov't dollars to pay
For roads, bridges, electric vehicles, internet usage, airports, research, and waterways

The excitement was huge as we stabilize to restore America for future generations to come
Chips in Science Acts 2022, returned supply chains and increased the tech edge some
It mandated the use of US made lumber, glass, and wood to revitalize industries stateside
<u>10 M</u> Americans who applied for small business loans, can now work together with pride

The Inflation Reduction Act credits electric vehicles to move forward w/in the clean air crisis
Big Pharma <u>lost</u> its cause of assisting sick by stuffing execs pockets with bonuses that enticed
#46 crusaded for billionaire companies be taxed 15% of earnings to reduce a $25T debt
#46 crusaded for the Junk Fee Prevention Act that <u>reduced</u> charges when travel was met

TRUMP

Proverbs 11:1
A false balance is an abomination to the Lord,
but a just weight is his delight

#45 exercised extreme influence over the operations of the Republican session
His racist approach to immigration, praised and shifted the GOP's aggressions
It evolved into a Maga "Party of Trump" w/norms exclusively about his "me"
His followers remained loyal to anything he said, even when they didn't agree

He idolized his dad, Fred Trump, who empire was worth $300M at death, in 1999
Fred Trump was on record of owning over 27,000 NY apartments at one time
Which sold later for 16 times its' previous worth, was the return they got back
Fred was arrested in 1927, at a KKK parade, and denied his rentals to blacks

#45 was the only President that refused to divulge his taxes as protocol dictated
Also, the only president who didn't attend the transfer of power in the states
His mishandling of the Covid virus resulted in 2.2M death due to failure to lead
He spewed mis and dis-info to citizens, as they scrambled emergently in need

A jury of 6 men and 3 women found #45 liable of sexual assault of a then young female
The Survivor's Law, created by BLM, empowered women to report, and rapist be jailed
She endured this assault w/ many consequences, and no legal support towards her defense
The judicial system gave credence to victims for a limited time, to report any sexual offense

TRUMP CRIMINALITIES

Proverbs 12:22
Lying lips are an abomination to the Lord,
But those who deal faithfully is his delight

#45 was infamously in a class of his own, the "rules of law" didn't apply to him
With no interest in the USA or world equality, he entered the race on a whim
The ex-reality star became intrigued with voters wanting someone different to vote for
The timing was perfect, he filled the gap, and walked inside of the White House doors

When asked how he managed to win, with no previous diplomacy or political skills
The inadequacies were apparent, when lies full of conceit began quickly to build
#45 gripped the presidency w/a disregard for policies and procedures in this nation
The full power made him want to rule forever, and became his only desired station

Manhattan, NY was the 1st state to indict #45 for falsifying records during a campaign
Charged also of inflating property values, and venues as security entitlements remained
In GA, a special investigation charged #45 with trying to overturn an election was done
In DC, a review continued re: #45 as the provocateur of the Capitol attack in year 2021

He was notorious for spouting untruths and landing suspicions on persons besides self
Using his presidential influence to intimidate cohorts was the hand he always dealt
#45 was never accountable for illegal activities including tax evasion was found
The rule of law protects rights from wrongs, except #45 always remained unbound

TRUMP and the DOJ

Mission statement

The mission of the Dept. of Justice is to uphold the Rule of Law, to keep our country safe and to protect civil rights ...

In August 2022, ex-President Trump Mar-A-Largo home was raid by the DOJ
Reason being was to secure and return White House classified docs #45 took away
An FBI warrant was presented to enter the home, #45 was clueless and out of town
This unprecedented call for action against #45, by the DOJ was about to go down

Authority to also extract add'l info re: the Jan. 6 seize on the capital was granted
Trump deemed the raid a political witch hunt, was what he continued to rant
The very next day, #45 was in NY courts on charges of falsifying property costs
He pleaded the 5th on each question asked of him, hoping the matter got tossed

His own lawyers confirmed 15 boxes of evidence were seized and taken away
Some regarding nuclear weapons matters, which posed constant threats everyday
This was a win for the public that day and reportedly Biden had not been informed
Biden reported he would run if Trump decided to run again and began to perform

Multiple agencies strategized and built criminal cases for years against Mr. #45
Delayed but not forgotten placed a light on democracy by keeping justice alive
The United States is at a serious crossroad where our democracy is being challenged
Simultaneously, the Senate agreed on little, as shootings remained a study imbalance

TRUMP IMPEACHMENTS

Proverbs 22:8
Whoever sows injustice will reap calamity and the rod of his fury will fail

#45, Donald J. Trump <u>was impeached</u> twice by legislators but without any convictions
For <u>Presidential Abuse of Power</u> and for <u>Obstruction of Justice</u> was the prediction
The Republics protected #45, and refused to convict due to fear and loyalty beyond belief
His hold on <u>their</u> future endeavors presented a narrative that <u>only</u> he was the <u>Chief</u>

He envisions a <u>world order</u> with an agenda focusing on his ideas and views alone
Like a dictator where citizens ideas met nothing, he alone was <u>King on the throne</u>
After evidence of wrong doings year after year, he was unscathed as others took the fall
In 2023, he was charged with falsifying records in a campaign year w/no one else to call

His personal attorney Michael Cohen, was imprisoned as an accessory to that <u>exact crime</u>
As #45 loyalty was to himself only, and placed many <u>cohorts</u> in prison time after time
He surrendered and traveled from Florida to a NY court to see if charges would stick
#45 pushed the law for decades, was found guilty, and the verdict came in quick

Found guilty on all <u>34 charges</u> by a NY jury of his peers, for influencing the 2016 election
Hush monies paid to Daniels, a porn star, reportedly had sex w/him sealed the connection
It occurred days before the election, to keep voters <u>uninformed,</u> he acquiesced to her demands
<u>$130K</u> paid by atty Cohen, and reimbursed by campaign funds is why the law took the stand

TRUTH IN OCOEE, FLORIDA

Proverbs 19:21
Many are the plan in a person's heart,
but it is the Lord's plan that will prevail

In 1920, community leader, July Perry, was murdered on an infamous day called "<u>Ocoee</u> <u>on</u> <u>Fire</u>
Before elections, Klansmen warned black communities if voted, consequences would be dire
Some Blacks made attempts unsuccessfully due to missing info and serious death threats
They were told to get the names of the deniers that night by at atty, for them to suffer regrets

Two police <u>killed</u> in a shuffle, by the hands of the white supremist, blamed the respected July Perry
Perry was pulled from his home, jailed, released, murdered, and hung for 4 days by the Klans query
They set homes, schools, and temples on <u>fire</u> and <u>shot</u> all blacks who sought their right to vote
This US savage massacre left over <u>300</u> <u>blacks</u> dead, due to a <u>false entitlement</u> claim they wrote

After <u>100 yrs.</u>, Ocoee residents want truth revealed, and reiterate mass dumping <u>is not a proper grave</u>
Students weren't aware of this historical fact, blocked by Gov. DeSantis of how Klansmen behaved
After 400 yrs. blacks have tried to make marks in their community, to get shot down and not succeed
Why do the powerful subjugate blacks, who <u>also</u> want a piece of the US pie to forwardly proceed

It's never too late for hatred, and entitlements to be <u>overruled by law</u> and begin to cease
Black & Brown Americans will be the majority race soon, decisions made by them will increase
Diversity, Equity and Inclusions (DEI) is not embraced universally to use Black ideas to give back
Modern day nationalist groups like Proud Boys and Neo Nazi, are ready, willing, and able to attack

TWENTY TWENTY-THREE (2023)

Ecclesiastes 7:8
The end of the matter is better than
its beginning and patience are better than pride

Twenty-twenty three (2023) arrived with many grateful to be above ground
Through thick and thin our supreme protector has allowed us to remain sound
We continue to believe good deeds will always trump over meanness and bad
Biden's 8.7% SSI increase for <u>7M retirees</u> after a decade, made <u>folks</u> feel glad

The worlds values and morals has changed faster historically than ever before
The <u>politics</u> of situations has become a front and center focus to make a score
Do not take criticism from people you would never seriously take <u>advice</u> from
Judge not the words but <u>actions</u> that represents who they <u>are</u> and <u>have</u> become

The global 2020 Pandemic displayed an enormous human ability and need to adapt
The 2021 attack on our Capitol provoked an investigation resulting in lots to unpack
The daily cost to live rose 7%, which was the US highest increase in over 40 years
As the rate of mass shootings also increased, the lack of <u>new laws</u> brought <u>new tears</u>

Scotus reversal of 1973 "Roe vs Wade's" right to give birth or abort was enacted
Scotus confirmed <u>Justice Ketanji Brown Jackson, the 1st black female judge</u> was adapted
Maryland is a state for safe abortions, with legal protection if that was the mothers' plan
Many states made abortion against the law, supporting any of #45 ideas, as his dying fans

An impact of carrying pregnancy to term can lead to poverty, hardship, and even evictions
Also, mental/physical health issues, domestic violence, chronic pain, and new addictions
Brittney Griner, a WNBA star, was released after 10 mo. in Russia for carrying some weed
The US granted more funds to Ukraine, against Russia's insatiable dishonorable greed

CALENDARIO 2023

TWO AMERICAS

Mark 3:24-25
If a kingdom divided against itself cannot stand, and if a house divided against itself, that house will be unable to stand

The vaccinated and the unvaccinated brought unknowing tears
Covid surpassed the deaths from the Spanish Flu in the 1918 year
675K deaths from the Spanish Flu, by Sept '21 680K from Covid 19
After a 100 years later, scientific technology has not fully gleaned

More people died in the <u>marginalized</u> state of Alabama than were <u>born</u>
Everyone knew someone who have passed, and populations are still torn
The right to say "<u>no</u>" affected everyone, including w/in the sphere of self
Conspiracies, and social media played a large part in jeopardizing health

New cases mounted and raged around the southern states
California the lowest, and Mississippi to date had the highest rates
The breakouts were concurrent w/flu season as children return to school
Parents gathered info to make a necessary decision, on how to safely rule

The unfinished war of <u>to or not to</u> vaccinate caused thousands of deaths
Toxic characters and lack of integrity assisted in a failure to do their best
The world wanted the pandemic to end, the <u>beast</u> was called "<u>Covid 19</u>"
The US was willing and able via the vaccine if all cooperated as a team

Many competed for limited hospital beds, as other illnesses were at stake
Covid occupied most hospital beds, when the new variances did self-create
Doctors had to make informed decisions as to who got the immediate care
Endless prioritizing of patients was non-stop, and a lot for Drs. to also bare

WAR

Galatians 3:28
There is neither Jew nor Greek, there is neither slave nor free,
there is no male and female, for you are all one in Christ Jesus

On 10/07/23, the Palestinian terrorist attacked Israel unexpectedly with an aim to kill
This was the 5th attack in 75 yrs. due to conditions and no action towards any goodwill
Israel had the money and resources and ceased all food, water, and electricity supplies
While continuing to bomb the innocent in communities where women and children died

America stood strong in support of Israel, as Palestinians humanitarian efforts reduced
Israel counter attacks asked citizens to flee homes before an Israel ground attack ensued
It was reported Hamas had 25 US hostages to use as leverage against the 14M Palestinians
The only solution was to negotiation and compromise this bone chilling catastrophic idioms

The world is divided as to when and why the fight originally began without apathy
Both countries want to have control over territories without the violence and tragedy
Many felt Israel presented crimes against humanity w/genocidal results and defenses
With no discussions or equitable conclusions, this long-term fight remained very tense

In 2022 Russia unprovoked attack on Ukraine set the bloodiest conflict in Europe since WWII
Economic, cultural, and political bonds now at an irreparable relationship, not being renewed
As history repeats itself, geo-political domination took over to obtain resources and power
As of 2024, the US has sent Ukraine $61B in military aid, to fight Russia who aim to devour

WITHDRAWAL

Romans 8:37
No, in all these things we are more than conquers thru him that love us, For I am convinced that neither death nor life, neither angels nor demons, neither the present nor the future, neither height or depths, nor anything else in creation, will be able to separate us from the love of God that is in Christ Jesus our Lord

...Selah

When the US under Pres. Biden, withdrew from a 20-year war in 2021
Isis-K bombed the airport killing 13 US men and 175 refugees with their guns
The" K "was for Kurricon: claimed responsibility as an extremist group since 2014
Out of frustration of the current failed regime, new extremist felt a need to be seen

Aircrafts dangerously flew into Kobel to get as many people as possible out
Gunfire into the massive crowds was what extremist were constantly about
Pres. Biden had a deadline for soldiers to leave by 08/31/21, with only weeks to plan
Previous presidents talked about ending the war, but #46 got it done and was the <u>man</u>

The Taliban released dangerous local prisoners to ramp up their military force
Over 17 extremist groups in 110 temperatures wanted supremacy and had no remorse
$300M? a day is what it cost America for assistance to a democracy we could not win
America had unprecedented amounts of projects to build, back, better and set to begin

Journalist and allies scrambled to secure papers to be accepted on the list to get out
85K out of 150K Pakistanis' and Americans left Kabul while others yelled in a shout
Lots of personal ties and complexities took place during the evacuation situation
20 other countries helped, as Britain and France requested more time in that equation